2018 EDITION

PRESENTED BY SHOWIT

SHOWIT

© 2018 Showit, Inc.
All rights reserved.

Visit our website at showit.co.

No part of this book may be used or reproduced in any manner without written permission from Showit, except in the context of reviews and sharing on social media.

All featured website content used by permission from the respective website owners and designers.

Copywriting: Cassandra Campbell, Jihae Watson
Design: Jed Smith, Nate Sees

ISBN 978-0-692-08890-6

Printed in China

INSPIRATION IS EVERYWHERE

AS LONG AS YOU KNOW WHERE TO LOOK

Lucky for you, we here at Showit have already done the looking for you, and what you now hold in your hands is a carefully curated collection of 50 websites that we feel confident will spark inspiration in you.

Couldn't you just view these beautiful websites in their natural habitats online? Of course you could, and in fact, we hope that at some point you will hop online and explore your favorites from this collection at greater length. But we also know that the online world is one of speed and distraction, and that the creative juices of our minds flow more freely when we step away from the cool blue lights of our screens.

So take your time and enjoy this look at work done by your fellow creatives. Admire the artistry, examine the details, decide what you like and don't like. Then find yourself dreaming about how you can craft your own website to reflect your unique personality and brand. Maybe someday it will be your work that sparks creativity in somebody else.

TODD WATSON
SHOWIT CO-FOUNDER / CEO

TABLE OF CONTENTS

Anchor & Veil	6
Jasmine Star	8
Gaby Caskey Photography	10
Lifeline Photography	12
Anna Taylor Photography	14
Jodie Brim Photography	16
The Ganeys	18
Suzy Goodrick Photography	20
Christine Lim	22
Lauren Kirkham Photography	24
Donal Doherty Photography + Film	26
Ike & Tash	28
Mariano Friginal Photography	30
The Wilds Photography	32
James & Jess Photography	34
Misty C. Photography	36
Ashlyn Writes	38
Kay + Bee	40
The Scobeys	42
Tarah Elise Photography	44
Suzanne Neace Photography	46
Matthew David Studio	48
Frozen Exposure Photo + Cinema	50
Brady Bates Photography	52
Sage Paper Co.	54

Mistry & Scott Photography	56
Leah Ladson Photography	58
Sarah & Dave Photography	60
Lemiga Events	62
Lauren Spinelli Photography	64
Vanessa Hicks Photography	66
Kate Supa Photography	68
Lukas Trudeau Event Co.	70
Tennison Weddings	72
Kristen Booth Photography	74
Alicia Yarrish Photography	76
Kevin DeMassio Photography	78
Emily Broadbent Photography	80
Jaimie Nicole Krause Photography	82
Leslie Herring Events	84
Traci and Troy	86
Jennifer Cole Photography	88
Kéra Photography	90
Chronicles Photography	92
Aura Elizabeth Photography	94
Casey Hendrickson Photography	96
Moriah Riona	98
Zack Deck Media	100
Courtney Aaron	102
Casey Chibirka Photography	104

ANCHOR & VEIL

🌐 ANCHORANDVEILPHOTOGRAPHY.COM

Devin and Kathryn have not only incorporated their bold and intimate brand into their online home, but a good bit of their contrasting personalities show up there, too! Almost opposite in every way (even artistic style) the photographers behind Anchor & Veil were able to thread themselves into the site seamlessly. With the help of the designers at Refinery Original, a "he said, she said" graphic portrayal turns a potentially boring "About" page into a personal encounter with both of them. Instead of a paragraph of their accomplishments, highlights of the couple's life together are presented in an elegant, visual timeline. By allowing the user to keep their eyes moving through the site with engaging graphics and bold images, visitors make a connection with Devin and Kathryn before they ever meet.

DESIGNED BY

ERICA CLAYTON
REFINERY ORIGINAL

REFINERYORIGINAL.COM

COLORS

#1A1A1A

#1E2428

#9F8162

#DBC795

#1E2D36

#485963

#F7F6F3

#FFFFFF

TYPEFACES

Bodega Script

Miller Banner

Cormorant Garamond Normal

Mossiatie

Playfair Display Normal

Miller Banner Italic

CINZEL NORMAL

Playfair Display Italic

Cormorant Garamond Light Italic

WE ARE ANCHOR AND VEIL

We are Charlotte Wedding Photographers and Our greatest desire is to combine our love and heart to create bold yet intimate images that evoke emotion. With the camera in our hand, we see the world differently than most and we would be honored to capture your wedding day in a bold, intimate, emotional way.

THIS HOPE WE HAVE AS AN ANCHOR OF THE SOUL, BOTH SURE AND STEADFAST, AND WHICH ENTERS THE PRESENCE BEHIND THE VEIL.
HEBREWS 6:19

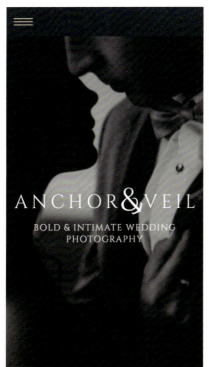

NEXT SET

JASMINE STAR

🌐 JASMINESTAR.COM

Starting as a photographer over a decade ago, Jasmine Star has taken all that she has learned from running a successful small business and made it into a business of its own. Helping entrepreneurs market and leverage their brand online and through social media, Jasmine knows a thing or two about what makes a website work. Through her collaboration with web designer, Promise Tangeman, Jasmine created a site that is more than her business details. "Are there a lot of people who help business owners grow their business on social media? Yes. But is there only one ME? Yes. I want my website to feel like a distinct representation, a snapshot, of how I could change a visitor's business. And life." Mission accomplished.

DESIGNED BY

PROMISE TANGEMAN
GO LIVE

GOLIVEHQ.CO

COLORS

#000000
#232323
#666666
#A0A0A0
#D5D5D5
#F2C8B6
#F6EFE8
#FFFFFF

TYPEFACES

Trade Gothic
Bodoni
Lato Light
Proxima Nova
Arapey
Playfair Display Italic
Proxima Nova Thin

JASMINE STAR

HOME
ABOUT
EDUCATION
REVIEWS
CONTACT
BLOG

BUILD THE BUSINESS OF YOUR DREAMS

JASMINE STAR

CREATE A BRAND

ABOUT JASMINE

Marketing, branding & building a powerful mindset for creative entrepreneurs.

I left law school, picked up a camera, pursued curiosity, and built the business of my dreams. A decade later, I educate entrepreneurs on how to do the same.

...

ABOUT

ABOUT JASMINE

EDUCATION   1/4

If you're on the cusp of doing something great with your business and you're committed to making it work, you may just need help figuring out what to do next. That's where I come in.

Together we'll make your dreams take flight, create a profitable business, and change your life in the process...

EDUCATION

01

REVIEWS

"She's a world-class marketer...it's her ability to share and connect with others on a personal level that really sets her apart"

- Photo Professional Magazine

REVIEWS

CONTACT JASMINE

If you have questions (or friendly love notes) about our products or services, email us at:

info@jasminestar.com

9

CONT

GABY CASKEY PHOTOGRAPHY

🌐 GABYCASKEY.COM

Though Gaby is only in her second year of shooting weddings, her site and photography would make you think otherwise. By scaling Davey and Krista's Bondi template to meet her professional yet fun vibe, Gaby Caskey has had no trouble attracting her dream client. With a playful brand voice that is very much her own, the streamlined layout of Gaby's site gives a healthy balance in contrast. Outside of the pop of her spunky logo, she has allowed her professionalism to take visual center-stage of her online storefront. It might be what attracts that potential client, but her joyful heart and belief that marriage is the most important part of any wedding day is what turns clicks into clients. And she turns those clients into friends. Just the way Gaby had always wanted her photography business to be.

DESIGNED WITH
BONDI BY THE PALM SHOP

COLORS

#040404
#4A4A4A
#E9D1A9
#2F4462
#F5F1ED
#FFFFFF

TYPEFACES

Raleway Normal
Raleway Bold
Bambusa Pro
Playfair Display Normal
Playfair Display Italic

ABOUT ME 01 | PORTFOLIO 02 | INVESTMENT 03 | REVIEWS 04 | CONTACT 05 | FAQS 06 | BLOG 07

hey hey!

My name is Gaby Caskey and I'm so glad YOU are here! I'm a portrait and wedding photographer living in San Antonio, Texas with my husband and sweet Dalmatian pup! Most days you can find me in yoga pants, an oversized t-shirt, and Chacos while drinking a Coca-Cola. No shame. Also, if you love the Office I'm pretty sure we'll be best friends forever.

SAY HEY »

OUR WEDDING DAY

WHAT I DO

I'm a portrait and wedding photographer serving San Antonio and the Dallas/Fort Worth area! When I'm not photographing others, I love playing with my nephews, planning out my next trip, or buying popcorn from the movie theater and having a Netflix marathon with my husband and pup!

I'M A FAN!
WHAT'S NEXT! »

LATEST ON
the blog.

06

LATEST ON
the blog.

SIGNATURE work.

JESSIE

SIGNATURE work.

bucket list

-Shoot a wedding where puppies are involved!! I didn't get my Dalmatian, Lexa, until *after* my wedding day so I've always wondered how I would've incorporated her into my special day!

-Shoot a wedding at the White Sparrow Barn...this was actually my wedding venue! From its perfect natural lighting to the beautiful outdoor area, it's definitely at the top of my bucket list!

-Shoot a mountainside ceremony as the sun sets. I love to hike, and golden hour is my favorite time to shoot, so it'd be a perfect combination!

NEWSLETTER

See my latest shoots, tips for sessions & where I'm headed. Coming soon!

LET'S WORK TOGETHER!
BASED IN FORT WORTH AND SAN ANTONIO, TX
hello@gabycaskey.com

ON instagram

PHOTOS BY GABY CASKEY | DESIGN BY THE PALM SHOP | SHOWIT

LIFELINE PHOTOGRAPHY

🌐 LIFELINEPHOTOGRAPHY.CO.UK

It is totally possible to smile when you enter a website for the first time. Whether it's the overjoyed smiles Hannah Webster captures, the pops of sunny yellow splashed on every page, or even the quirky font and arrows navigating your eyes, it's impossible not to feel the playfulness of lifelinephotography.co.uk. Hannah wanted her online home to be true to who she is in real life. With the help of the Melissa Love from The Design Space, Hannah makes it clear, in bold font, what she believes, and who her ideal client is. She even teases the user to find out if her hair is really pink by clicking on the next page. Inviting engagement at every scroll. "People know exactly who I am and what I am offering before they even meet me because the site says it all. I'm converting more enquiries as a result." And it all started with a smile.

DESIGNED BY

MELISSA LOVE
THE DESIGN SPACE

THEDESIGNSPACE.CO

COLORS

#000000

#F7F7F7

#FFFFFF

#FADD4B

#CEB53B

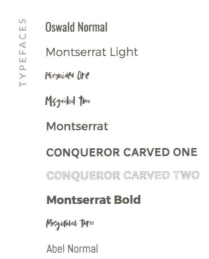

TYPEFACES

Oswald Normal

Montserrat Light

Misguided One

Misguided Two

Montserrat

CONQUEROR CARVED ONE

CONQUEROR CARVED TWO

Montserrat Bold

Misguided Three

Abel Normal

ANNA TAYLOR PHOTOGRAPHY

🌐 ANNATAYLORPHOTOGRAPHY.COM

The instant you find Anna Taylor's online storefront, you are greeted by the photographer's brilliant smile from behind the desk of her office. With such a warm welcome, it isn't long before you feel like you have just met for coffee with the owner of Anna Taylor Photography. After meeting Andra and Kelly, the designers behind With Grace & Gold, everything fell into place. This North Carolinian photographer breathes life into every image she shoots. So when it came to creating her website, Anna ensured it had just the right balance of light, timelessness, and joy. It is undeniable that Anna is focused not only on the details of shooting a wedding, but the long term goals of the couple, as well. It is clear to potential clients that Anna cares for their journey through marriage. Her images and the heart behind her business are focused on the legacy her photography can capture which easily conveys through her gorgeous site.

DESIGNED BY

KELLY ZUGAY & ANDRA BARKEY
WITH GRACE & GOLD

WITHGRACEANDGOLD.COM

COLORS

#333333

#888888

#C9D8DF

#E9EFF4

#C0D4D0

#D3BA98

#F9FBFB

#FFFFFF

TYPEFACES

Fifi
Freight Big Pro Light

MEDIA GOTHIC

Acre

JODIE BRIM PHOTOGRAPHY

🌐 JODIEBRIM.COM

Attention to detail can really set the stage for booking your ideal client. Jodie of Jodie Brim Photography is a prime example. Her site sticks to a light and romantic color palette that flows so thoroughly through her branding that you will even find it in all of her images. Her airy font and photos whisk you from one portrait to another, while the visitor basks in the timeless and elegant feel of the site. Jodi's well-thought-out branding has paid off. "I've been able to book clients just from them seeing my website and without even speaking on the phone like I normally would. It's helped to build trust and confidence within my potential clients and it's a pretty good feeling when we do actually meet and they say you're exactly how I imagined." With Jodie's fine-tuned branding and The Coop Marketing's design skills, JodieBrim.com is serving as a perfect online storefront.

DESIGNED BY

COLBY STELLHORN
THE COOP MARKETING

THECOOPMARKETING.COM

COLORS

- #7F8287
- #F7D5CB
- #DDE3E3
- #C4BBB8
- #EDEBE6
- #C5AD6A
- #F9E3DC
- #FFFFFF

TYPEFACES

Copperplate Light

Brisbane

Libre Baskerville Normal

Playfair Display Italic

THE GANEYS

🌐 THEGANEYS.COM

Tuscany? South Africa? Peru? It is impossible to determine the location of the romantic venues The Ganeys take you to upon entering their site. Though based in Florida, the romantic and adventurous heart of Emily, and her husband Thomas, are instantly relayed to attract clients who share their same ideals. While the photographers focused on "capturing authentic moments", Ravyn of Three Fifteen Design focused on conveying the same message through the design elements of their online home. "Our website finally showcases who we are. It allows us to stand out in the best kind of way. It has provided us with a platform to show off our couples and attract new ones with the same ideals and principles. Our new website has been so much more than that though, it has given us courage and confidence."

DESIGNED BY

RAVYN STADICK
THREE FIFTEEN DESIGN

THREEFIFTEENDESIGN.COM

COLORS

#363636

#636363

#9A9A9A

#91976B

#C3C7B5

#E0E1D7

#EEEEEF

#FFFFFF

TYPEFACES

TRUE NORTH

Northwell

Old Standard TT Normal

Old Standard TT Italic

Old Standard TT Bold

WEDDING PHOTOGRAPHY
for ADVENTUROUS LOVE

01. VIEW THE GALLERIES
02. MEET EMILY & THOMAS
03. CONNECT WITH US

Our Single Wedding Package

As your photographers, our priority is taking the best photos possible, which is why we created our one wedding package with you in mind.

LEARN MORE ABOUT THE EXPERIENCE

follow along: @THEGANEYS

THE GANEYS
Wedding Photography
Florida • USA • Worldwide

GALLERIES   ABOUT US   INFORMATION   BLOG   CONTACT   ▲ BACK TO TOP

© THE GANEYS 2017 | BRANDING BY THREE FIFTEEN DESIGN

SUZY GOODRICK PHOTOGRAPHY

🌐 SUZYGOODRICK.COM

It would be easy to let the photography speak for itself. Suzy Goodrick has a full portfolio depicting her dream clients. Welcoming visitors with one of her romantic desert shoots, she pairs the image with these words, "intimate wedding photography for the free spirit." Working with the team at Go Live, Suzy was able to apply her desire for minimal navigation, natural elements, and a touch of geometric design to her online home. "Trusting the creative process was the most crucial decision when preparing for the new site. When clients inquire, I'm confident they know and trust my brand; there's no second guessing if we're the right fit for one another. I truly believe my website has launched my business into a season it otherwise would not have experienced." And her constant flow of inquiries is proof of that.

DESIGNED WITH
NOTORIOUS BY GO LIVE

COLORS

#000000
#4B4B4B
#828282
#BB9155
#E4D1B5
#F0F0F0
#E2D5CF
#FFFFFF

TYPEFACES

PT Sans Italic
Raleway
Raleway Thin
PT Sans Normal
Raleway Light

SUZY *goodrick*

INTIMATE WEDDING PHOTOGRAPHY
FOR THE FREE SPIRIT

HOME | GALLERIES | MEET SUZY | INFO | BLOG | CONTACT

@SUZYGOODRICK

COLLECTING MOMENTS
YOU'LL ADORE.

FOLLOW
@SUZYGOODRICK
ON INSTAGRAM

ENGAGEMENTS

SUZY *goodrick*

INTIMATE WEDDING
PHOTOGRAPHY FOR THE
FREE SPIRIT

Let's embrace the wild in us.

Fierce freedom. It's not about having all the right things in the right places, but letting the details fall where they may. Embracing the natural. I'll capture the moments that sweep you away. Whether it's through the desert, mountainous fields, or on city sidewalks, we'll trek this journey together to tell a story that is uniquely and unapologetically you.

Located in Phoenix, AZ

f ⊙ ⓟ

more →

CHRISTINE LIM

🌐 CHRISTINELIMPHOTOGRAPHY.COM

Since her first camera in the 4th grade, Christine Lim has been capturing feelings, friends, and all things in between. After earning a degree in Creative Photography, she never thought she would find herself in the wedding world. And that's exactly what is conveyed through Christine's online home. She is a wedding photographer for the couple who prefers a more minimal and honest approach to capturing their wedding. While a bevy of romantic florals might look out of place at ChristineLim.com, a touch of feminine blush here and there reminds prospective clients she is still all about love. Splashing a bold font across her intimate images balances out the loveliness with a clever pop, thanks to Jeff and Jen of Tonic Site Shop. The site comes all together to reinforce Christine's desire to show people how beautiful their life is.

DESIGNED WITH
LEMON DROP BY TONIC SITE SHOP

COLORS

#404041
#F4E2D5
#E9C2B8

#FFFFFF

#C4C2BF
#DFDEDA
#F7F6F3

TYPEFACES

Oswald
Montserrat
Ubuntu
Crimson Text Italic
TREND SANS

HELLO!

So happy that you've found me. I know the internet is a big place and there is no shortage of talented photographers in Toronto or the world, for that matter.

So please, take a look around and if you find yourself connecting with my images, I would love to grab a coffee in person (or FaceTime!) and get to know you, your story and your plans.

xo
Christine

LEARN MORE

MEET ME · BROWSE MY WORK · READ THE BLOG · GET IN TOUCH

FOLLOW ME ON INSTAGRAM
@CHRISSYLIM

CHRISTINE LIM

HOME · PORTFOLIO
ABOUT · EXPERIENCE
BLOG · CONTACT

REAL LOVE.
REAL MOMENTS.

I'm a Toronto-based photographer, with a love for telling real love stories: authentic, honest and all you.

LAUREN KIRKHAM PHOTOGRAPHY

🌐 LAURENKIRKHAMPHOTOGRAPHY.COM

Striking a balance between "experienced professional" and "compassionate confidant" is no easy feat. As a Family and Newborn photographer, Lauren Kirkham feels it is a necessity for her job. Documenting real moments of everyday life, the ups and the downs, are seen in every image on her site. The first shot of a family in PJs still in bed is an almost subconscious reminder that Lauren is a trustworthy family advocate, and compassionate confidant. Conveying that she is an experienced professional shines through in the sleek layout and design, thanks to fellow New Yorker, Christina Laing of The Buffalo Collective. Together they were able to express Lauren's love of life and knowledge that children are always a gift at LaurenKirkhamPhotography.com

DESIGNED BY

CHRISTINA LAING
THE BUFFALO COLLECTIVE

THEBUFFALOCOLLECTIVE.COM

COLORS

#1A1A1A

#3E3E3E

#616161

#7C7C7C

#AEAEAE

#C9C9C9

#F5F5F5

#FFFFFF

TYPEFACES

Lora

Montserrat

Josefin Sans Normal

Cormorant Garamond Normal

Oswald Light

01	02	03		04	05	06
HOME	ABOUT	PORTFOLIO	LAUREN KIRKHAM	INFO	CONTACT	BLOG

LAUREN KIRKHAM

FAMILY + LIFESTYLE

photography

SCROLL FOR MORE

documenting your family's legacy

I believe in the power of printed photographs. These are family heirlooms that tell the story of your life and its many stages. From childhood, to falling in love, to parenthood and the family that you grow into together.

LAUREN KIRKHAM

FAMILY + LIFESTYLE

photography

MEET LAUREN

I am a wife and a mama who lives to capture natural moments of love, joy, crazy and quiet.

VIEW THE IMAGES

A collection of our favorite moments, captured and preserved in time.

BOOK A SESSION

Let's chat about all the special details! I can't wait to meet you and your family.

documenting your family's legacy

DONAL DOHERTY PHOTOGRAPHY + FILM

🌐 DONALDOHERTY.COM

To some, natural and fun might seem like the direct opposite of timeless and editorial. A tall order, but Donal of Donal Doherty Photography + Film had dreamed up the perfect way to express these ideals to his potential online clients. "An editorial feel was really important, we aimed to make the experience feel like they were reading a fashion magazine." With the website expertise of his friend Melissa Love of The Design Space, Donal is able to showcase his relaxed photographic style in images and video, through crisp composition . "It's been amazing to showcase the progress in the business. We've gone from most potential clients booking photography to booking a collection including film and photo both."

DESIGNED BY

MELISSA LOVE
THE DESIGN SPACE

THEDESIGNSPACE.CO

COLORS

#39313D
#818BA4
#444444
#8DC2BF
#E2CDC7
#F5F5F5
#F9F9F9
#FFFFFF

TYPEFACES

Lato Light
Lato Normal
Playfair Display Normal
Didot
Playfair Display Italic
Open Sans Normal
Raleway Normal
Montserrat Normal

DONAL DOHERTY

HOME · ABOUT · EXPERIENCE · PHOTOGRAPHY · FILMS · PHOTOBOOTH · CONTACT · BLOG · EDUCATION

DONAL DOHERTY
PHOTOGRAPHY + FILM

natural, fun, editorial

PHOTOGRAPHY + FILM

You've fallen in love, said 'Yes!' and now you're planning the wedding of your dreams. Our team of fine art photographers and film-makers will capture

natural, fun, editorial

PHOTOGRAPHY + FILM

You've fallen in love, said 'Yes!' and now you're planning the wedding of your dreams. Our team of fine art photographers and film-makers will capture the story of your day in a natural, fun and authentic way, ensuring you'll have memories to cherish for eternity.

Based in Ebrington Square in the heart of Derry, Northern Ireland, I've spent the last seven years chasing light and capturing love in Ireland and around the world. Our award-winning customer service and storytelling through photography and film, and our photo booth experience, has enabled the team to offer an unrivalled experience for couples.

MEET THE TEAM →

WELCOME

ready to
EXPLORE?

our PORTFOLIO

PHOTOGRAPHY

WE CAPTURE
carefully crafted heirloom images

VIEW

FILMS

WE CREATE
a timeless cinematic record

VIEW

IKE & TASH

🌐 IKEANDTASH.COM

How do you attract your ideal client when you don't specialize in one particular genre of photography? Isaiah and Latasha Haynes made the decision early on in their business that there was a simple answer: "We decided to put the focus on us and what we love to do and who we are and less on the services we provide. That worked really well in communicating our brand." In other words, IkeandTash.com is based on…Ike and Tash. Following with their brand, when you hit their site, the first thing you see is the stylish couple, and their beautiful daughter, Wisdom. With a click or a scroll, the angled images create lines leading you through the site and all it has to offer. Angles, clean fonts, and a modern black and white base helped designer Erika Clayton of Refinery Original, lift Isaiah and Latasha's imagery off the screen, bringing life to the couple's words. The site "tells our story and it tells it in a really full and comprehensive way."

DESIGNED BY

ERICA CLAYTON
REFINERY ORIGINAL

REFINERYORIGINAL.COM

COLORS
- #000000
- #19191A
- #D9BD85
- #FFFFFF
- #7C7878
- #E7E7E7

TYPEFACES
- Raleway Normal
- Libre Baskerville Normal
- Old Standard TT Italic
- Libre Baskerville Italic
- Playfair Display Normal
- Playfair Display SC Normal
- Raleway Light
- Old Standard TT Normal
- Open Sans Normal
- Open Sans Light

HOME   ABOUT   PORTFOLIO   BLOG   THE STREET TEAM   AND HER SOUTH SOUND   BLINK CONFERENCE   EDUCATE   SHOP   CONTACT

1.
ABOUT

Hey there! We're Ike & Tash, wedding and portrait photographers based out of the beautiful Pacific Northwest. We focus on weddings and engagements, high school seniors and families, but that's only half the story. We're also passionate about sharing, investing and growing the industry, and that's why we've worked so hard to offer educational resources and experiences for our fellow photogs and entrepreneurs. One of our biggest endeavors is BLINK, our annual boutique conference for photogs of all kinds that focuses on empowering, networking and providing leadership...so that we all can grow our business dreams into realities.

Thank you for stopping by and checking us out. We're pumped that you stumbled across our little piece of the World Wide Web and hope that you'll hang for a while. So kick back, look around, and if you like what you see – send us a little love note. We're thrilled that you're here and cannot wait to connect with you!

-Ike and Tash

We specialize in sassy, bold, edgy and urban lifestyle portraiture. We adore candid moments, love moments, LIFE MOMENTS & we breathe air to capture them. Enjoy as we give you a peek into our CRAZY world!

[ABOUT US AND OUR PASSION →]

2.
PORTFOLIO

3.
THE STREET TEAM

1.
ABOUT

Hey there! We're Ike & Tash, wedding and portrait photographers based out of the beautiful Pacific Northwest. We focus on weddings and

29

MARIANO FRIGINAL PHOTOGRAPHY

🌐 MARIANOFRIGINAL.COM

Several, if not most children learn to create art from an early age. Not many though, learned the art of creative entrepreneurship as early as Mariano Friginal. As a kid, he sold his sketches to friends for covers of their school binders. Today, he is still capturing images but traded in his pencil for a camera. Stopping by his online storefront, visitors will see his lifetime of artistry transcend every image. A rotating gallery corresponding to each menu option informs potential clients that no matter which specialty they are here for now, they will be back for more later. Pouring life into each still image, visitors will learn quickly from his galleries to his portfolio, and even layered background images, Mariano will handle each moment and detail with special care, like only a true artist could.

DESIGNED FROM SCRATCH
IN SHOWIT

COLORS

#000000
#2F333A
#636363
#E85049
#046280
#C2C3C8
#ECEBE8
#FFFFFF

TYPEFACES

Mr Eaves XL Mod Heavy

Mr Eaves XL Mod Heavy

Industry Demi

Industry Book

Park Lane Light

Open Sans Light

Source Sans Pro Light

Josefin Sans Light

"Art has no survival value; rather it is one of those things which give value to survival."

– C.S. LEWIS

As a kid, I remember sketching Star Wars characters fighting with the Transformers on for ten bucks a piece. Fast forward to the present — I still get to do what I love (minus

THE WILDS PHOTOGRAPHY

🌐 **THEWILDS.PHOTOGRAPHY**

With a passion to build self-esteem and bridge community gaps amongst high school seniors, Alison Faulkner knew she had to stand out in an oversaturated market to succeed. When designing an online home to attract her "wildly unique" client, she started with the most straightforward way available to her, a video of a typical shoot. With a catchy tune in the background, the viewer is immediately taken into the fun video. Short in length, the scrolling happens instantaneously. Alison's light and airy images pop off the pink and white background only to be rivaled for attention by the adorable images as a visual guide to any questions you may have about the process. With customizations by Swoone, and Alison's clear vision and heart behind The Wilds Photography, every Senior will be asking their parents for a Wild shoot!

DESIGNED WITH
MASON BY SWOONE

COLORS

#353533

#A78F78

#FEEFEA

#E0E0E1

#F5F5F6

#FFFFFF

TYPEFACES

Oswald Normal

Montserrat Light

Old Standard TT Italic

Jacques Gilles

Montserrat Normal

Old Standard TT Bold

Old Standard TT Normal

PIROU

MENU

LET'S CHAT

THE WILDS
photography

couture senior photography & videography for

The Wild at Heart

01 UNMATCHED **02** ABOUT ALISON **03** THE BLOG **04** GALLERIES **05** PRO HMUA **06** INVESTMENT **07** REVIEWS

THE WILDS
photography

THE MOST SOUGHT AFTER SENIOR PORTRAIT EXPERIENCE IN BLOOMINGTON, INDIANA

Offering all-inclusive, exclusive, couture photographs and films that are only achieved by focusing solely on high school seniors. You are unique and you deserve a photographer who is dedicated to your once in a lifetime senior portrait experience. The Wilds Photography speaks to those who appreciate unsurpassed quality, personalized style and gorgeous images that perfectly define you at this turning point in your life.

WHY CHOOSE THE WILDS

couture senior photography & videography for

The Wild at Heart

I THINK SENIORS ROCK

And I'm really good at celebrating awesome moments with dance parties.

about alison

33

JAMES & JESS PHOTOGRAPHY

🌐 JAMESANDJESS.COM

As bi-coastal wedding photographers, James and Jess had a tall feat of appealing to laidback clients in California and elegant east-coasters in New York. To make it really tricky, the website also needed to reflect James and Jess's fun and approachable personalities. In their words, the site needed to be "luxury with open arms." Working with designer Jeffrey Shipley, they were able to find the balance mixing old world style with light and airy imagery. In website terms, Jeffrey paired a neo-classical crest created as the photographer's logo overlayed on a sunny California bridal shot. With cheeky copy, and the adorable couple with wide grins on every page, JamesandJess.com will have couples on both ends of the continent asking the photographers to reserve their wedding dates years in advance.

DESIGNED BY

JEFFREY SHIPLEY
J. SHIPLEY CREATIVE

JSHIPLEYCREATIVE.COM

HIGH-CONTRAST SERIF
IN ALL CAPS FOR TITLES

THE J&J LOVE STORY

ELEGANT SCRIPT
FOR SUBTITLES

Adventurers. Storytellers. Best Friends.

TIMELESS SERIF WITH EXTRA
KERNING FOR BODY COPY

Hello there! We are James and Jess Wittmayer, a pair of best friends who fell in love thanks to photography and reality TV. There was also an important make-out session in a movie theater, but we digress...

We met shortly after James moved to Santa Barbara (Jess' hometown) to attend Brooks Institute of Photography. Jess was already an established wedding photographer and he noticed Jess while she was taking photos at church ...

PHOTOGRAPHY *for the* JOYFUL, CLASSIC, MADLY IN LOVE COUPLE

Begin the Journey

JAMES & JESS

SANTA BARBARA   NEW YORK CITY

Established 2006

Hi, friends. We are James & Jess –Husband & Wife traveling coastal city dwellers based in Santa Barbara and New York City. Every place we find ourselves becomes, for as long as we both there, home.

We are deeply in love with each other, and we take that love with us as we photograph and educate everywhere we go. We are complete extroverts who value deep relationships. This makes community really important to us; we need it, we believe in it, so we create it. We are community-minded, traveling adventurers who take world class, iconic photos and never, ever stop laughing.

GET TO KNOW US >

READ *the* BLOG   HOME   BROWSE GALLERIES   ABOUT US   Be Social
                  THE J&J EXPERIENCE   EDUCATION   SAY HELLO

Browse the
WEDDINGS
Open Galleries

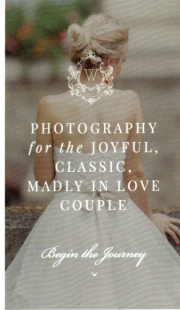

PHOTOGRAPHY *for the* JOYFUL, CLASSIC, MADLY IN LOVE COUPLE

Begin the Journey

THE J&J LOVE STORY

Adventurers. Storytellers. Best Friends.

MISTY C. PHOTOGRAPHY

🌐 MISTYCPHOTOGRAPHY.COM

Down to earth with a little bit of sparkle, that's what you get when you come across MistyCPhotography.com. This online home is a perfect reflection of the photographer in real life. Misty knew her ideal client was much like her. "Fun, likes a little bit of adventure, and generally is engaged!" Through working on her site with Louise, the designer behind The Autumn Rabbit, the two came up with a romantic and stylish layout. "It gives clients a professional view of my business, and it's intuitive, and beautiful!" Keeping the images light and glowing, the graphic overlays classic, with a fun photographic arrangement of Misty's loves, any viewer would be drawn to learn more about Misty C Photography. And that's exactly what they are given a chance to do with a fun video of the engaging photographer behind the gorgeous images.

DESIGNED BY

LOUISE ROSS
THE AUTUMN RABBIT

THEAUTUMNRABBIT.COM

COLORS

#1E1E1E
#3C3C3C
#676767
#A1A1A1
#687B81
#F6F6F6
#D0D6D9
#FFFFFF

TYPEFACES

Old Standard TT Italic

Open Sans Italic

Vidaloka

Open Sans Normal

Open Sans Light

Adelicia

Open Sans Semi Bold

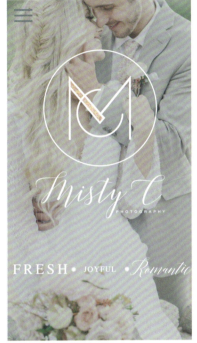

ASHLYN WRITES

🌐 ASHLYNWRITES.COM

First time online customers decide quickly if they will stay or go when they hit a website. As a veteran of the modern marketing world, copywriter Ashlyn Carter knew she could not rely solely on her well-honed wordsmithing to entice internet visitors to stay awhile. Instead, she made herself accessible from the instant a potential client opens Ashlyn's webpage without a word. This clever copywriter created a short, pieced-together group of clips of behind the scenes footage. The fly-on-the-wall video keeps viewers intrigued, removes their finger from the mouse, and get's them reading every creative word. Designed with the desire of "getting great words to great women," Ashlyn's website is a bevy of information and inspiration.

DESIGNED WITH
JACK ROSE BY TONIC SITE SHOP

COLORS

- #000000
- #313541
- #96A7B7
- #A7A9AB
- #D4C0D2
- #F6F0EE
- #EDECE8
- #6B6B6B

TYPEFACES

- Raleway Normal
- Libre Baskerville Normal
- Bickham Script
- Old Standard TT Italic
- Montserrat Normal
- Sorts Mill Goudy
- Libre Baskerville Italic
- Old Standard TT
- Ubuntu Medium

THERE'S A LOT OF NOISE OUT THERE.

Freshly sharpened pencil bouquet ready, I'm here to make sure *you stand out.*

Hi, y'all! I'm Ashlyn Carter, and I support my dreams (and our two German Shepherds) as a copywriter for creatives and calligrapher.

Here, you'll work with a someone who gets it—I've been where you are, both as a bride and a business owner: find out how to focus on what matters as you build your legacy, steward your gifts, and tell your story.

Throw your hands up and say yeah—or just pour a French 75 (mind pouring me one too, while you're at it?). Let's do this.

Select from 2 ways to wordsmith

ARE YOU A CREATIVE & NEED

COPYWRITING

Need words that fly in formation? Get marketing copy & messaging for your creative business, so you can start making magic (*and* money).

< START HERE

ARE YOU A BRIDE & NEED

CALLIGRAPHY

Dreaming up a hand-calligraphed wedding suite that'd pair well in a silver frame post wedding bells? I'd love to serve you!

START HERE >

TRUSTED BY

KAY + BEE

🌐 KAYXBEE.COM

Bringing a fun and modern twist to an editorial style could be what sets the Ashleys, the photographers behind KayxBee.com, apart from the crowd. However, it's really the photographers behind the style that helps viewers to engage. With the design savvy of Jenna Johnson of White & Salt, newcomers are welcomed to the site with full-screen images of warm and vivacious wedding shots. These set the professional tone like a firm handshake paired with a friendly smile. The Ashleys immediately reaffirm that tone by not only sharing a map of places they have been, and want to go, but their 2017 goals, many of which they have accomplished, and others are still in the making. By pairing their obvious talent and vulnerability of dreams to aspire to, their website visitors will think, "these are the photographers I need for my wedding, and friends I have been missing in my life."

DESIGNED BY

JENNA JOHNSON
WHITE & SALT

WHITEANDSALT.COM

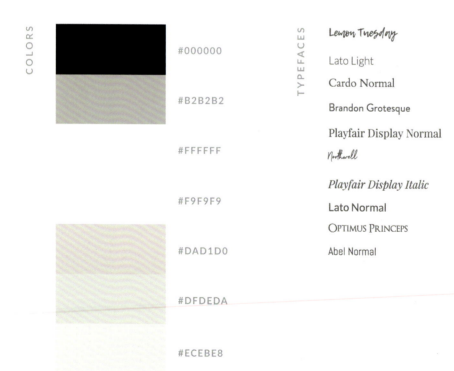

COLORS
- #000000
- #B2B2B2
- #FFFFFF
- #F9F9F9
- #DAD1D0
- #DFDEDA
- #ECEBE8

TYPEFACES
- Lemon Tuesday
- Lato Light
- Cardo Normal
- Brandon Grotesque
- Playfair Display Normal
- Northwell
- Playfair Display Italic
- Lato Normal
- OPTIMUS PRINCEPS
- Abel Normal

HOME • ABOUT • PORTFOLIO • FOR BRIDES   KAY×BEE   FOR PHOTOGRAPHERS • CONTACT • *read the blog*

WE HAVE A PASSION FOR
wild love + traveling

WE HAVE A PASSION FOR
wild love + traveling

MEET THE ASHLEYS

favs

our WORK

WEDDINGS
ENGAGEMENT
DETAILS

FUN AND
stress free

You know those beautiful wedding photos you see on Pinterest? Well, those are the wedding photos you'll receive if you book Kay & Bee! not only is their photography stunning, these girls is a beautiful inside and out! They made planning fun and stress free because they know the questions to ask to make sure the day runs smooth. Also, having two photographers allows you to get two perspectives from your big day! That's pretty wonderful and a no brainer if you ask me! Remember, you get what you pay for. Splurge on Kay & Bee. You won't regret it.

EMILY

OUR LATEST
news

41

THE SCOBEYS

🌐 THESCOBEYS.COM

Moving from Atlanta, Georgia to the mountains of Colorado, meant having to move to a new wedding market for Ashley and Graham Scobey. TheScobeys.com would remain a place to connect to people with big hearts and easy-going natures, but now they were hoping to attract couples with adventurous spirits, too. Putting their new business ideas in the hands of designer Jeffrey Shipley was their first step. "We created a fun trail-map menu, and then used custom iconography throughout to tie it all together. Further, we wanted the design to also feel super minimal and clean so that their work and copy would remain the focal point." With Jeffrey's well-thought-out design and The Scobey's vision, they have been booking "the right kind of clients" ever since.

DESIGNED BY

JEFFREY SHIPLEY
J. SHIPLEY CREATIVE

JSHIPLEYCREATIVE.COM

NAVIGATION ELEMENTS

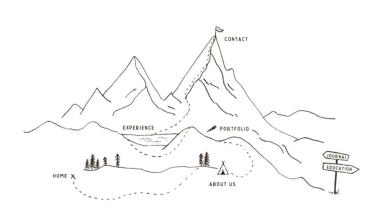

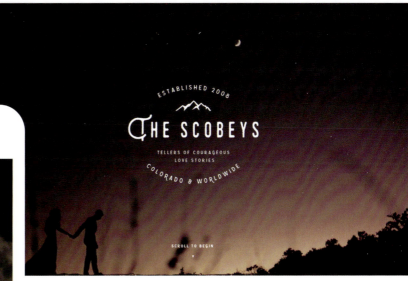

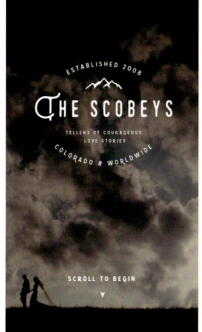

HI, WE ARE
THE SCOBEYS

we are so glad that you have arrived here. our site is a reflection of how we view life. it has twists and turns and maybe a surprise or two if you look for them. go on an adventure, get lost for a moment, and don't worry - you can always find your way back. get in touch when you are ready. your love story is exceptional, your photos should be, too.

WHO WE ARE

This is where our relationship starts! We are going to ask you to trust us. To give us a backstage pass to your love story. It's only fair that you get a backstage pass to ours. Let's get to know each other. This is going to be the beginning of something beautiful.

get to know us

TARAH ELISE PHOTOGRAPHY

🌐 TARAHELISEPHOTOGRAPHY.COM

With the rotation of images introducing the viewer to Tarah Elise's photographic style, one gets transported into each romantic scene. Working with her amazing designer friends from With Grace & Gold, Tarah's site makes you believe you are watching a French film rather than scrolling through a wedding photographer's site. Whether a couple is planning an adventurous wedding in the mountains, or by the sea, or even tucked away in a chalet in the Swiss countryside, they all hold the same truth for Tarah: they are fun-loving adventurers that are bound to be her next client, and will indefinitely choose to be her next friend.

DESIGNED BY

KELLY ZUGAY & ANDRA BARKEY
WITH GRACE & GOLD

WITHGRACEANDGOLD.COM

COLORS

#000000
#19191A
#2D453D
#5E4F39
#C09B3C
#BD8D89
#ECEBE8
#FFFFFF

TYPEFACES

Brat

Roman Bold Italic
Roman Bold
Din Breit
Roman Italic
Batik
Manus

Roman Regular
Dubiel

TARAH ELISE
· PHOTOGRAPHY ·

MY FIELD NOTES

BEFORE ADVENTURING WITH ME, YOU SHOULD KNOW:

I'm a love story photographer

FOR THE

adventurous hearts.

01 — I married my hunk of a husband on the rainiest day in October - and it was absolutely magical.

02 — We have two Boston Terriers - Chuckles and Giggles - so yea, we spend a lot of time laughing in marriage and in life.

03 — My couples become like family to me - in fact, I still text regularly with so many of my brides!

04 — My passport is always ready for the next adventure. Some of my bucket-list destinations include Greece, Ireland, and New Zealand!

05 — I'm a huge advocate for mental health and taking care of yourself - I talk more about it on my personal lifestyle blog, Bloom and Wander.

WHEN I'M NOT ADVENTURING, I'M FOUND HERE -

explore the
Wedding Experience
Finding cozy spots off the beaten path, driving with the windows down, and marrying the love of your life.

I'LL CAPTURE IT ALL. →

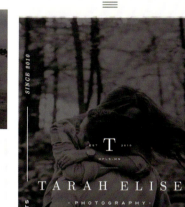

SWEET WORDS — FROM CLIENTS

She felt more like an old friend than a hired photographer.

- SAMMIE, BRIDE

01
A WASHINGTON MOUNTAIN ANNIVERSARY SESSION · SEATTLE, WA
VIEW POST

02
A BOHEMIAN STYLE MINNESOTAN SUMMER WEDDING
VIEW POST

03
A MINNESOTAN TAYLORS FALLS ENGAGEMENT · NORTHERN MINN.
VIEW POST

SUZANNE NEACE PHOTOGRAPHY

🌐 SUZANNENEACEPHOTOGRAPHY.COM

The images of Seniors rotate on the screen with the scripted words "modern and authentic" placed next to them. This intentional pairing helps you to understand the purpose behind Suzanne Neace's photography business. In fact, as the font shrinks, the viewers will be drawn to the message that stands alone on SuzanneNeacePhotography.com: "Where the focus is on capturing you: the ultimate work of art." Through each section of Suzanne's site, her images of young teens peering into the camera really lets the viewer know these Seniors are completely comfortable with themselves, and their photographer. With a light and naturally-toned online storefront, Suzanne shares a bit about her process, and herself, recalling how she wished she could do her senior pics over and then inviting her audience to not make the mistake she did.

DESIGNED WITH
SMOKESCREEN BY TONIC SITE SHOP

COLORS

#D8DEDE
#3A3A3C
#D7D1C5
#A6A6A4
#FFFFFF

TYPEFACES

Notera
Muli Normal
Libre Baskerville
Lato Light
Libre Baskerville Italic
Playfair Display Normal
Adobe Garamond Pro Italic
Lato Bold
Playfair Display Italic
TREND SANS
Lato Normal
Knockout
Muli Light
Prata Normal

Modern & Authentic

Senior Portrait Photography

WHERE THE FOCUS IS ON CAPTURING YOU: THE ULTIMATE WORK OF ART

About

I don't want to be hired to take a picture. Anyone can do that. I want to get to know you, learn what makes you tick... and then capture who you are, not just what you look like.

SUZANNE NEACE PHOTOGRAPHY BEGAN WITH THE DESIRE TO BRING MY SON'S STORY TO LIFE IN THE MOST AUTHENTIC WAY POSSIBLE.

Utilizing my bachelor's degree in Studio Art (see Dad... I told you it would come in handy someday!) and a little bit of blind faith I started my journey into high school senior portrait photography in 2011. Focusing on those who challenge the status quo, who aren't afraid to be who they are, and using my camera to document their unique high school experience.

YOU ARE ONE-OF-A-KIND.

YOUR PHOTOGRAPHY EXPERIENCE SHOULD BE TOO.

Awesome personalities deserve more than just pretty pictures... and lasting memories only ever come out of unforgettable experiences. That's what I'm here for: to make this fresh and fun.

The end result? Authentic expressions of your true self. No manufactured moments. Just you: comfortable and confident in your own skin. I already love what I see in you. Now it's your turn.

When I'm not working with my awesome clients, I also manage a chaotic household of seven, dream of competing in another triathlon someday, and occasionally belt out Broadway show tunes in the car where no one else can hear me.

If I could re-take my senior pictures I'd ditch the big 80's hair, the corny studio backdrops, and staged poses. I'd head to the coolest urban location I could find wearing my skinny jeans, black boots, and favorite UO cardigan.

Where will your senior portraits take YOU? Get in touch and let's find out.

Modern & Authentic

Senior Portrait Photography

I am an artist... and a professional

AS AN ARTIST I UNDERSTAND LIGHT AND KNOW HOW TO USE IT. AS A PROFESSIONAL PHOTOGRAPHER I KNOW WHAT LENSES, CAMERA CONTROLS, AND SOFTWARE WILL GIVE YOU THE BEST IMAGES POSSIBLE.

NEXT >

MATTHEW DAVID STUDIO

🌐 MATTHEWDAVIDSTUDIO.COM

She wasn't looking for bells, whistles, or "a lot of doo-dads". Christina Frary, of Matthew David Studios, wanted their images to standout on their own. So, when creating the website with the wonderful design minds at Foil and Ink, Christina drew from a simple format the studio follows as a whole: "We consider our creative vision to be whimsical, dreamy, & nostalgic, while staying true to the natural chemistry of the moment." They bring the viewer into their unique desert paradise from the beginning with their desert landscape image to fill the screen, to the full portrait image that just teases those clients to keep scrolling. The art of David Matthew Studio whisks you through to the very end when you are treated to the grand finale of a recent wedding captured in 8 mm film.

DESIGNED WITH

ATHENA BY FOIL & INK

COLORS

#000000

#4D4D4D

#727272

#455A4D

#DDD6C4

#B5B7AD

#ECEBE8

#FFFFFF

TYPEFACES

Fjalla One

Montserrat

Lato Light

Playfair Display

Cardo Italic

| NO. 1 | NO. 2 | NO. 3 | NO. 4 | NO. 5 |
| ABOUT | INFO | IMAGES | BLOG | CONTACT |

MATTHEW DAVID STUDIO

Welcome to our little space. We are fine art wedding and portrait photographers in Palm Springs, California, who live in the moment, are perpetual wanderers, and who long ago fell in love with the art behind the photographic image. Stay a spell, check out our work, and say hello....

NO.1
LOVE

NO.2
LIFE

NO.3
FAMILY

NO.4
CINEMA

FROZEN EXPOSURE PHOTO + CINEMA

🌐 FROZENEXPOSURE.COM

A splash of color, a dash of glitter, and some very merry clients is the recipe for the brilliantly festive online storefront of FrozenExposure.com. The owners, Tanya and Bobby Macks, went to Rachel Earl Design with a desire for a site that was not a direct reflection of their personalities, but of their ideal couple. "Our ideal client dreams big, gets butterflies over the small things, and believes there is beauty in every moment." Nothing says dreamer like glitter that pops-up when you roll your mouse over each button, or confetti that just happens to fall in the perfect shape of a unicorn. These little details will have you playing with the site, but it's the professionally playful images that will make you stay. Party on the outside, but professional on the inside. Now that's a recipe for success.

DESIGNED BY

RACHAEL EARL
RACHAEL EARL DESIGN

RACHAELEARL.COM

COLORS

#EEACB2

#F19EA6

#FFFFFF

#6D6D6D

#EEB586

TYPEFACES

Crimson Text Italic

PT Serif Normal

Lato Light

Quicksand Light

Fjalla One

Montserrat

PT Serif Italic

PLAYFAIR DISPLAY SC NORMAL

Aterism Bold

Cantoni Basic Normal

Lora Normal

Cantarell Normal

IM Fell French Canon Normal

Crimson Text Normal

Lora Italic

MEET THE TEAM

WEDDINGS

PORTRAITS

PHOTOBOOTH

SEND US A NOTE

READ THE JOURNAL

51

BRADY BATES PHOTOGRAPHY

🌐 BRADYBATESPHOTOGRAPHY.COM

As one of the youngest professional photographers in his area, and possibly the country, Brady Bates is anything but green. To showcase his free-spirited photos, Brady needed a professional, yet unconceited online home that spoke to his ideal client's heart. When creating his website, using a design by Tonic Site Shop, he had an ample selection of images to attract adventurous couples who "aren't afraid to get a little muddy and have wind blown hair on top of a mountain." With so many natural elements playing a role in his photography, the elevated simplicity of Brady's website is the exact match needed. His homepage reads like a heartfelt letter instead of the technically perfect portfolio that it is. BradyBatesPhotography.com is the perfect reflection of the experienced and young photographer it represents.

DESIGNED WITH
GIN FIZZ BY TONIC SITE SHOP

COLORS

#231F20
#414042
#E7E8E9
#FFFFFF
#C4C2BF
#F9F9F9

TYPEFACES

Baskerville Italic
Montserrat Light
Oswald
SACKERS GOTHIC
Baskerville
Playfair Display Italic

☰ MENU

BRADY BATES
PHOTOGRAPHY

HOME   ABOUT   GALLERIES   DETAILS   CONTACT   BLOG

ADVENTURE IN THE SHENANDOAH MEADOWS

WELCOME

I like to get creative, shoot photos and climb mountains in the process of it all.

read more

WELCOME

I like to get creative, shoot photos and climb

AS SEEN IN

FREE PEOPLE
social media

VIRGINIA LIVING
magazine

THE KNOT
storefront

FEATURED

SKYLINE DRIVE SESSION

sunset session hiking at shenandoah national park, virginia

view gallery

MEET BRADY

I BELIEVE IN THE LIFE WELL-LIVED

My goal is to capture moments as they happen, the authentic behind the scenes photos. The little moments that carry deep feeling. I want to photograph your relationship for what it truly is.

read more

FEATURED BLOG POSTS

COUPLES   WEDDINGS   COUPLES

LAUREN & JUSTIN   **KATE & LEVI**   **CAROLINE & BRIAN**

view post   *view post*   *view post*

THE GALLERIES

EXPLORE MORE ADVENTURES

explore the portfolio

53

SAGE PAPER CO.

🌐 SAGEPAPERCO.COM

If a girl can leave all she knows to follow her heart to live among the mountains, a successful business doing what she loves is completely in her wheelhouse. Using her founding principles of "the belief that wisdom, love and grace are stronger when shared," Alexa Behar started a business, Sage Paper Co., dedicated to creating timeless art to help brides, and the creative at heart, celebrate their most important events. Alexa wanted to create an online storefront that reflected the heart behind her art. Taking a page from her time spent in Tuscany, SagePaperCo.com is like a slow walk down cobblestone roads. With crisp, airy shots of her work as a watercolor artist and calligrapher, Alexa introduces her potential clients to elegant style deeply rooted in her natural surroundings.

DESIGNED WITH
BETHANY BY THE PALM SHOP

COLORS

#040404
#4E4E4E
#C5B8A8
#E7D9CE
#EDEBE6
#C9C9C9
#FFFFFF

TYPEFACES

Libre Baskerville Normal

Crimson Text Italic

Crimson Text Semi Bold

Libre Baskerville Italic

Crimson Text Semi Bold Italic

Crimson Text Bold

Montserrat Bold

Crimson Text Normal

Montserrat Normal

Lora Italic

Libre Baskerville Bold

Sage
PAPER CO.

BESPOKE WATERCOLOR & CALLIGRAPHY

instagram facebook pinterest

I	II	III	IV	V	VI	VII	VIII
HOME	ABOUT	PORTFOLIO	SERVICES	SHOP	WORKSHOPS	JOURNAL	CONTACT

Sage
PAPER CO.
BESPOKE WATERCOLOR & CALLIGRAPHY
EST. 2015

hi friend,

I'm Alexa Behar, the hands and heart behind Sage Paper Co. Born in Chapel Hill, North Carolina, and raised on a farm outside Nashville, Tennessee, nothing speaks to my heart quite like southern hospitality. With this hospitality comes genuine love, intentionality and grace. I am a firm believer that the proper combination of these three things—both in my lifestyle and my designs—enriches the soul and fosters joy. My hope is that you use my designs to live more intentionally, love more fearlessly and extend grace in all circumstances.

the full story →

wedding
INVITATIONS + DAY OF DETAILS

art prints
WATERCOLOR + CALLIGRAPHY FOR YOUR HOME

cards
STATIONERY FOR EVERY OCCASION

THE SHORT & SWEET

CHRISTINE & CURT,
SPC COUPLE

MISTRY & SCOTT PHOTOGRAPHY

🌐 MISTRYANDSCOTT.COM

If you searched for a Seattle photographer and came across Mistry and Scott's website, you would be happily surprised by the bright and natural light infused in every image. The husband and wife duo desire to capture moments of joy-filled love, and thus, choose that to be reflected through their website. With clean lines, a classic font, and the design help of Jason Toevs, the photos of authentic moments are able to shine and focus on the the client experience. "We are obsessed with the client experience and focus our talents on great image quality and equally on relationships that endure past the actual event or occasion we are photographing." By drawing their inspiration from real client experiences, Mistry and Scott are able to make those images work overtime on their website, allowing their visitors to get to know the real them.

DESIGNED BY

JASON TOEVS
JASONTOEVS.COM

COLORS

#000000
#333333
#4F6470
#EAD9A2
#74BABA
#B3B3B3
#ECEBE8
#FFFFFF

TYPEFACES

Cantarell
Cantarell Bold
Playfair Display
Playfair Display Bold

HOME GALLERIES MEET US RAVES **MISTRY & SCOTT** PHOTOGRAPHY -EST. | 2012- INVESTMENT CONTACT BLOG

GALLERIES

ENGAGEMENTS   WEDDINGS   SENIORS   FAMILIES

SEE MORE FROM THE MISTRY & SCOTT BLOG

WE ARE A HUSBAND & WIFE PHOTOGRAPHY TEAM SERVING SEATTLE AND BEYOND!

Choosing the right Seattle Wedding Photographer can be difficult. We take a very limited amount of weddings each year to be able to focus 100% of our attention to each of our clients. The two of us have built a successful marriage of over 20 years, and we know what it takes to endure. We love to see engaged couples start their journey of marriage off on the right footing.

We pride ourselves in taking beautiful timeless images that showcase that wedding day in a very authentic way...making sure we take care of documenting every element and detail, while also focused on creating a romantic and elegant day that's about the two of you together! We want you to remember the smells, the feelings, the emotions of what this day is about...the love you have for one another.

We also want you to enjoy your wedding photographs for decades and for future generations to come, that's why we include an album in every collection we offer. The last thing we want is for your images to live on a hard drive somewhere in the back of a desk collecting dust.

We serve the entire Seattle Puget Sound area, and often photograph weddings in Skagit, Whatcom, and Snohomish Counties. We love to travel for that Eastern Washington Estate or Winery Wedding, or to the San Francisco Bay Area for weddings in the Livermore Valley, Pleasanton, Danville and Alamo. Just know...no distance is too far for us! As experienced Seattle photographers we are here to walk you through this process from beginning to end. We look forward to hearing all about your wedding day!

MISTRY & SCOTT PHOTOGRAPHY -EST. | 2012-

GALLERIES

LEAH LADSON PHOTOGRAPHY

🌐 LEAHLADSON.COM

Leah Ladson is one of those photographers that can do it all. The problem she kept running into was how to put it all into a well-designed website. So, when it came time to reflect on how to appeal to all her clients without compromising on design or her minimalist eye, she enlisted the help of Morgi Mac Design. Together they decided to attract new clients from the many areas she serves by creating two balancing visual elements. Clean-lined black text boxes and soft splashes of pink throughout the site allow a juxtaposition of soft and bold elements. By choosing graphic elements that support the photographer's craft and audience, it allows Leah's images to take center stage. A well-balanced site shifts potential clients to focus on Leah's visual storytelling that is the real reason to book her immediately.

DESIGNED BY

MORGAN MACDONALD
MORGI MAC

MORGIMAC.COM

COLORS

#000000
#FAD9D2
#636363
#ECECEC
#FFFFFF
#DFDEDA
#ECEBE8

TYPEFACES

Oswald Normal
Oswald Light
Fjalla One
Lato Bold
Lato Light

HI THERE
I'M LEAH LADSON

I am one of Bendigo's leading photographers providing the highest quality imagery of your love, life and business. I am also the founder of Girls From The Go, Bendigo's own support network for women in business. If you are looking for a wedding photographer, family photographer or need some commercial or product photography, just take a look at some of my previous clients to get a feel for what I can create for you.

SARAH & DAVE PHOTOGRAPHY

🌐 SARAHANDDAVEPHOTOGRAPHY.COM

From the second you land on their homepage, the bright and cheerful images of Sarah and Dave Photography will draw you in. However, it will be the details that keep potential clients scrolling and clicking their website with the desire to connect further with the couple. From the recollection of Sarah's favorite photos she keeps going back to in her own life, to the the clever layout of images of favorite things, and the playful ampersand connecting their names, this website is all about the little things that turn an online business into a an online home. While designers, Davey and Krista Jones, created so many of the site's elements with the intention to attract "laid back couples that still love details," their focus on Sarah & Dave is what will turn visitors into clients.

DESIGNED BY

DAVEY & KRISTA JONES
DAVEYANDKRISTA.COM

COLORS
- #585858
- #FEE092
- #E1B7AE
- #F9DAAF
- #E9B775
- #DFEEEF
- #FFFFFF

TYPEFACES

Montserrat Italic

Montserrat Light

Sorts Mill Goudy Italic

Montserrat Medium

Montserrat Ultra Light

Montserrat Bold

Montserrat Normal

Sorts Mill Goudy Normal

HOME · MEET US · WEDDING PHOTOGRAPHY · OUR PORTFOLIO · THE BLOG · GET IN TOUCH

welcome friends!

We're a husband and wife wedding photography team, capturing love stories through bright, joy filled, authentic images. We're so glad you've stopped by. We can't wait to meet you!

LET'S EXPLORE TOGETHER
think of it like us welcoming you into our home.

get to know
SARAH & DAVE

We're husband and wife wedding photographers, and while our photography takes us all over the east coast, we're based right in the heart of the city we adore, in Richmond Virginia. We somehow manage to love exploring new places and the latest restaurants just as much as we love staying in for a home cooked meal and a relaxed game night with friends.

meet us properly over here
grab a drink, get cozy, and stay a while!

welcome friends!

We're a husband and wife wedding photography team,

GETTING *married?*

Our goal is to photograph every wedding with the care and focus with which we would want our own wedding to be photographed. And that starts with an amazing experience with us from the very beginning until way after your wedding day is over. We've created a first class S&D wedding photography experience for you that is full of special treats and exceptional service and care, that is truly unlike anything else. We'd love to tell you all about the process!

what it's really like to work with us

FEATURED ON THE BLOG
our favorite weddings in richmond & beyond!

LEMIGA EVENTS

🌐 LEMIGA.COM

To say Lemiga Events is just an events planning company would be a gross understatement. If you know Michelle Gainey, the mastermind behind Lemiga Events, then you might start to have some idea. Luckily, the web designer behind Carrylove Designs was able to combine all the elements of Michelle's business into an elegant version of a "choose-your-own-adventure" book. With a high-end clientele of busy, fashionable professionals, Lemiga.com needed to be straight-forward and creative at the same time. With areas to direct potential clients to seperate areas of the site for event planning or lifestyle inspiration, time is never wasted. With a feed from Michelle's YouTube channel, viewers are even invited to stay and watch or come back next week for a new video. And with Michelle's smiling face greeting you, why wouldn't you?

DESIGNED BY

AMANDA SHUMAN
CARRYLOVE DESIGNS

CARRYLOVEDESIGNS.COM

COLORS

- #021119
- #F8F7F5
- #BA3731
- #A31F55
- #F7A5A1
- #DEC292
- #FFFFFF

TYPEFACES

Cormorant Medium Italic

Cormorant Medium

Spinwerad

Avenir Next

LET GO OF THE
DETAILS
ENJOY THE JOURNEY

Lemiga Events is an Atlanta based boutique company specializing in full service planning and event design. We craft luxe celebrations for savvy clients who crave to go beyond what's familiar and expected for their special event. Our clearly defined planning process allows you to enjoy the journey and let go of feeling overwhelmed and stressed.

MEET MICHELLE

CHOOSE YOUR JOURNEY

PLAN YOUR EVENT
OUR SERVICES
Let's talk about how we can guide you every step of the way for your event.
START HERE

GET INSPIRED
LIFESTYLE
Your resource for adding a little magic to everyday life with creative ideas and tips.
START HERE

NEW VIDEOS EVERY WEEK
YOUTUBE
SUBSCRIBE NOW >

My YouTube Channel is all about finding the balance between the simplicity of daily events and the art of stylish, meaningful celebrations. I aim to inspire you - despite your busy life - in creating memorable everyday life experiences, which are the heart of growing cherish relationships.

LAUREN SPINELLI PHOTOGRAPHY

🌐 LAURENSPINELLI.COM

While some may think a photojournalistic approach to wedding photography may seem dull, LaurenSpinelli.com shatters that misconception. The fun script of the owner's name is lightly splashed across a fast-paced moving reel of images packed with emotion. Should you get caught staring, there is a little arrow with a lighthearted suggestion to "just keep scrolling." Visitors will no doubt continue down to the bold yet simple font alerting you to her main goal in capturing your wedding, "Let's keep it candid." And every photo gallery image completely backs up this statement. Desiring an online storefront that allowed her images to breath and have the ability to stand on their own, Lauren Spinelli has created a clever showcase of her work and subtle nods to her fun-loving personality.

DESIGNED WITH
HARLOW BY THE BUFFALO COLLECTIVE

COLORS

#151515

#3E3E3E

#AA9883

#7C7C7C

#AEAEAE

#C9C9C9

#F5F5F5

#FFFFFF

TYPEFACES

Raleway Normal

Brandon Grotesque

Raleway Italic

Montserrat Normal

Oswald Light

VANESSA HICKS PHOTOGRAPHY

 VANESSAHICKSPHOTOGRAPHY.COM

Upon arriving at VanessaHicksPhotography.com, one will be immediately swept away to the paradise island she calls home. This Hawaiian photographer has mastered the art of bringing her natural surroundings into images, as well as her enchanting branding laced throughout her online home. Starting with a logo that speaks whimsy and not pretension, potential clients will be captivated by Vanessa's romantic images of couples, and playful family beach memories preserved. Vanessa has made her story and heart known through the pages of her site. With soft botanical elements, a light palette, and clean font choices, potential clients know they are in good and talented hands.

DESIGNED WITH
BREVE BY REFINERY ORIGINAL

COLORS

#7C7870
#68655F
#D8A5C2
#F7EDE7
#A0A2A0
#E8ECE9
#FFFFFF

TYPEFACES

Libre Baskerville Normal
Cormorant Garamond Normal
Lato Light
Quicksand Light
Libre Baskerville Italic
Antler Light
Cormorant Garamond Italic
Montserrat
wilderness
CINZEL NORMAL
Mutton Two
Lora Normal
Playfair Display Italic
Quicksand Normal
Cormorant Garamond Light Italic

KATE SUPA PHOTOGRAPHY

🌐 KATESUPA.COM

Early in her business, Kate Supa realized the key element to a beautiful image was due largely to clients that felt comfortable being photographed. "I quickly realized that people want to see and know the person behind the camera." While that becomes somewhat easy to do via social media platforms, Kate went to the Go Live intensive workshop to ensure she and her brand would shine through her website, as well. With a black and white minimalist design, KateSupa.com allows potential clients to get to know her photographic style. Light lines direct the viewer's eye to the image geared to her "In love, happy, and full of life" clientele. Heavy borders and thick layers of text cause Kate and her work to pop off the screen, engaging any passerby to stay just a bit longer.

DESIGNED BY

PROMISE TANGEMAN
GO LIVE

GOLIVEHQ.CO

COLORS

- #000000
- #D4C1B4
- #F0E4DB
- #636363
- #F0F0F0
- #F2E9E5
- #F7F2F0
- #FFFFFF

TYPEFACES

Fjalla One

Montserrat

Lato Light

Montserrat Bold

Bentham Normal

Playfair Display Normal

ABOUT
WORK
REVIEWS
CONTACT
BLOG

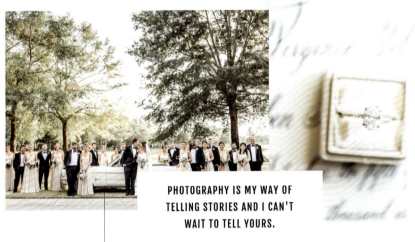

PHOTOGRAPHY IS MY WAY OF TELLING STORIES AND I CAN'T WAIT TO TELL YOURS.

ABOUT KATE

I wake up every morning with a full cup of coffee and a full heart knowing that I've got the best job in the world. I've built the business of my dreams and it keeps getting better because of people like YOU.

Creating beautiful photos of people with beautiful souls is my jam. I can't dance or sing but I can bring to life the wedding of your dreams through my photographs.

VIEW WORK

LUKAS TRUDEAU EVENT CO.

🌐 LUKASTRUDEAU.COM

If someone just happens upon LukasTrudeau.com, it won't be long before they will be planning an event for the sole purpose of having this creative duo work their magic. A modern website in navigation, Leslie Lukas and Angela Trudeau's event images are given their moments to shine so potential clients can really put themselves into each moment. With the help of Stacey Townsend of Townsend Collective, a clean layout guides the viewer through rustic moments in their native Colorado, on to elegant botanical works of art created exclusively for their high-end clientele, visitors will spend their time at the Lukas Trudeau Event Co. online home dreaming of how to work one of their events into the calendar.

DESIGNED BY

STACY TOWNSEND
TOWNSEND COLLECTIVE

TOWNSENDCOLLECTIVE.COM

COLORS

#101D26
#344538
#617764
#EFF0F1
#5C2931
#E1D1C4
#F2F2ED
#FFFFFF

TYPEFACES

Cormorant Garamond Normal
Cormorant Garamond Semi Bold
Cormorant Garamond Italic
Pinyon Script Normal

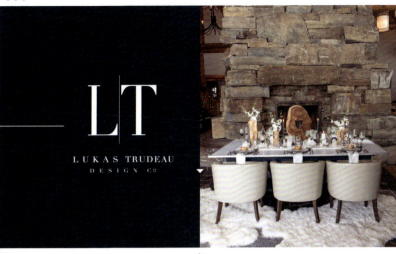

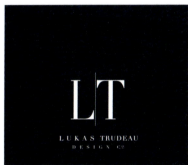

TENNISON WEDDINGS

🌐 TENNISONWEDDINGS.COM

When you create ethereal wedding videos like the Tennisons do, those films need to be front and center when a potential client happens upon your site. To ensure the cinematic events are not mistaken for run of the mill wedding videos, angled graphic elements are added to frame and highlight the spotlighted film of the moment. With simple navigation and straightforward story paths, even little gems like a hidden logo suddenly appearing on screen when scrolling, can add to the magic of Justin and Kelsey Tennison's online home. They know their ideal client is "someone who truly values video and the creativity and time it takes." The couple also can feel assured and laidback when it comes to their wedding day, knowing their memories are in the hands of complete professionals.

DESIGNED WITH
BUTLER BY THE AUTUMN RABBIT

COLORS

#151515
#363B41
#848585
#ADADAF
#836C4D
#A38A61
#423626
#F6F6F6

TYPEFACES

Amiri Bold Italic

Amiri Bold

Amiri Normal

Amiri Italic

League Script Normal

Source Sans Pro Normal

Source Sans Pro Light

Kaufmann BT

KRISTEN BOOTH PHOTOGRAPHY

🌐 KRISTENBOOTH.NET

Photographer Kristen Booth and Designer Julie Story paired up for this site design because they are both professional creatives with one thing in common: both truly believe that fairytales do come true. Over 2 years of brainstorming, followed by 3 months of design work from Julie, resulted in this one magical site. Home of all things whimsical, KristenBooth.net is an enchanting site where true romantics will get lost. With images that are best described as "warm, dreamy and other-worldly," photographer Kristen Booth loves shooting in arena that has old-world charm. Her attention to detail and magnifying who her couples are via her website has already paid-off. "Within a month of launching it, I booked a destination wedding at a chateau in France!" Now that's magic!

DESIGNED BY

JULIE STORY

julie-story.com

COLORS

#7C7870
#68655F
#D8A5C2
#F7EDE7
#A0A2A0
#E8ECE9
#FFFFFF

TYPEFACES

Monsieur La Doulaise Normal
Nixie One Normal
Lora Normal
Lora Italic
Giuliettas
Foglihten
Giulietta

75

ALICIA YARRISH PHOTOGRAPHY

🌐 ALICIAYARRISH.COM

It can be scary to plunge into being a full-time small business owner. As Alicia Yarrish took the plunge, she threw all her ideas over to the designer at The Autumn Rabbit, Louise Ross, to get the look she couldn't put her finger on. She trusted her images and branding to the right hands. Not only does Alicia's site delight in the details, there is no design element left neglected. Knowing Alicia has an enthusiastic zest for life, Louise incorporated some playful colors and surprising navigation that pair so well with the light and elegant images from the photographer. With pops of peach throughout the site, AliciaYarrish.com allows visitors to know the photographer is "sophisticated and never stuffy". The perfect balance any bride would enjoy having as part of her special day.

DESIGNED BY

LOUISE ROSS
THE AUTUMN RABBIT

THEAUTUMNRABBIT.COM

COLORS

#F1F2F4
#545859
#B4BFC7
#E0E5E9
#FFFFFF
#F1ECE9
#FDDAC5
#F79A7B

TYPEFACES

Anglecia Italic
Anglecia Regular
Lato Light
Lato Light Italic
Old Standard TT Italic
Fillo

ALICIA YARRISH

international wedding & anniversary photographer

I'M ALICIA

AN EN VOGUE INTERNATIONAL WEDDING AND ANNIVERSARY PHOTOGRAPHER.

A fun and authentic lifestyle photographer passionate about creating family heirlooms for your great great grandchildren. An artist creating fine art travel photographs to inspire wanderlust across America and abroad.

WHAT'S YOUR *Story?*

IN LOVE PROPOSAL ENGAGED
WEDDING ANNIVERSARY NEWBORN

SWEET *Words*

77

KEVIN DEMASSIO PHOTOGRAPHY

🌐 KEVINDEMASSIO.COM

There is a familiarity to the style of KevinDeMassio.com. With clients "who enjoy some of the finer things in life, but don't take themselves too seriously," the couples he works with are people you have known your whole life or maybe you saw them in a magazine recently? On his site, Kevin's rich imagery sets him apart, yet somehow makes him relatable as well. Framed between all this elegant beauty lies an adorable image of him and his family. Paired with his sweet words about loving his roots and familial role, visitors know they will be able to relax when they step in front of his lens. And maybe that's what seems familiar about Kevin's images. When showcased on his crisp, minimalist online home, his vibrant photos stand out. That's when it becomes clear, he isn't just shooting clients, but capturing new friends' memories.

DESIGNED WITH

VERTICAL BY DESIGN SPACE

COLORS

#000000

#19191A

#4B5665

#70BEBB

#A0D4D2

#DFDEDA

#F9F9F9

#FFFFFF

TYPEFACES

Lato

Lato Light

Montserrat Normal

Fjalla One

Libre Baskerville Italic

KEVIN DEMASSIO

HOME BLOG ALBUMS PORTFOLIO PHOTO BOOTH FAMILY SITE CLIENTS CONTACT

WELCOME TO
KEVIN DEMASSIO

ABOUT — GET TO KNOW ME

PORTFOLIO — VIEW THE IMAGES

THE BLOG — LATEST POSTS

ABOUT ME

Every couple I've been lucky enough to meet have been unique, and have had their own ideas and beliefs about their ideal wedding. One thing that all of my couples have had in common, however, was the goal of finding the perfect photographer that would best represent them and their family while beautifully capturing their wedding.

My promise is to capture your wedding in the most stunning fashion, all while creating an environment in which it's safe to be yourself. One of the first steps of feeling comfortable on your wedding day is building a relationship with your photographer. By inviting couples to meet in person at my studio, I am able to hear your story, listen, and find out what is most important to you. From there I am easily accessible and eager to answer any wedding related questions you may have. I am constantly working on building a relationship with my couples, so come wedding day, it's like working with a friend. The only way to truly achieve this, is by getting to know you. Your wedding is about you, your family, and your friends. To capture it would be an honor.

TESTIMONIALS

THE FIRST STEP TO AMAZING IMAGES IS GETTING TO KNOW YOU

PORTFOLIOS

EMILY BROADBENT PHOTOGRAPHY

🌐 EMILYBROADBENT.COM

With a light and airy feel to all her images, Emily Broadbent desired her online home be an extension of the joy she captures. No bold colors or heavy font fell onto Emily-Broadbent.com at the hands of Sofia Boyer from Magnolia Creative Studio. With a subtle cascade of flowers running under and through layers of images and text, one barely notices how this botanical illustration helps guide the viewer's eye from one part of the site to the next. With images layered on top of images, the potential client receives a full sense of all the beautiful moments Emily will capture for their future wedding day. With a sweet "random facts" about Emily done in a stylish font, clients will already be picturing her by their side on their wedding day.

DESIGNED BY

SOFIA BOYER
MAGNOLIA CREATIVE STUDIO

MAGNOLIACREATIVESTUDIO.COM

COLORS

#040404
#A09D98
#DED6D3
#F3E7E1
#EDEBE6
#D3C8C4
#FFFFFF

TYPEFACES

Libre Baskerville Normal
Montserrat Light
Old Standard TT Italic
Libre Baskerville Italic
Washington
Playfair Display Italic
Montserrat Bold
Montserrat Normal
Libre Baskerville Bold

BEHIND THE LENS

It's about more than just taking pictures

I believe the entire experience should be effortless, memorable and fun!

I'm a St. Louis wedding photographer, that loves capturing light, love and joy. My specialty is in telling your unique love story though bright, airy, timeless images.

PROVIDING YOU WITH AN INCREDIBLE PHOTOGRAPHY EXPERIENCE

JAIMIE NICOLE KRAUSE PHOTOGRAPHY

🌐 MODERNSTLPHOTO.COM

One of the qualities photographer Jamie Krause looks for in her ideal client is their willingness to get dirty and readiness to venture down questionable alleys for the perfect shot. This might terrify some potential clients to not even view her work. But they would be missing out for sure! When visitors stumble upon Jamie's online home, they know following her anywhere for a great shot would be the most riskless decision they ever have to make. Her work, modern photojournalism, and fine art, stand out quickly on her online portfolio. Her site, "simple, image focused, clean, and modern," lets visitors know they won't have to sweat the small details. Jamie will take care of it all. And knowing from her tongue-in-cheek copy, your time together will be laid back and so much fun.

DESIGNED WITH
PIONEER BY NORTHFOLK

COLORS

#000000
#303030
#AAAAAA
#F4F4F4
#E5E5D9
#FFFFFF

TYPEFACES

Amiri Bold Italic

Amiri Bold

Amiri Normal

Amiri Italic

League Script Normal

Source Sans Pro Normal

Source Sans Pro Light

Kaufmann BT

LESLIE HERRING EVENTS

🌐 LESLIEHERRINGEVENTS.COM

In order to draw a distinction between themselves and the relatively saturated market of wedding and event planners, Leslie Herring Events desired their online home to be sophisticated, yet completely approachable. They took their ideas to the designers at With Grace & Gold to ensure they were appealing to couples "interested in celebrating their love story through meaningful events." The website and branding took on a timeless quality through images, words, and layout. The logo with the firm's initials is in dark contrast to the light palette of their brand and images, which makes it pop off the screen. But the playful script tones it down, and visitors will know they can place their wedding in these friendly, capable hands.

DESIGNED BY

KELLY ZUGAY & ANDRA BARKEY
WITH GRACE & GOLD

WITHGRACEANDGOLD.COM

COLORS

#000000

#19191A

#D9D9D9

#EEE8E0

#EEDDC9

#E5C6B7

#204E45

#FFFFFF

TYPEFACES

Old Standard TT Italic

Old Standard TT Normal

Josefin Sans Light

Josefin Sans Normal

Playfair Display Italic

LESLIE HERRING
EVENTS

HOME   ABOUT   SERVICES   GALLERY   JOURNAL   CONTACT

LESLIE HERRING EVENTS

―――

An award-winning and nationally praised wedding planning firm and team of professional celebrators. Serving brides from New York to Texas, our passion is telling love stories through meaningful celebrations.

― WHERE PLANNING MEETS ―
innovation

MEET OUR TEAM

VIEW OUR SERVICES

VIEW OUR WORK

SWEET CLIENT PRAISE

ERIN & JOE

"Leslie, Thank you for being the most patient, calm, and detail-oriented wedding planner of all time! You always handled me and all our vendors with unparalleled professionalism. Thank you for making sure all the details were handled; you put me at ease because I knew you were all over it! I appreciate all the hours you put in for my big day(s). The wedding turned out even better than I expected - please thank your team for me! Thanks for everything."

PREVIOUS / NEXT

TRACI AND TROY

🌐 TRACIANDTROY.COM

With a collection of fun-loving and polished, though completely genuine images, Traci and Troy needed a website that complimented their style. This brother and sister team approached designing their website the same way they introduce themselves to new clients: friendly and with a genuine enthusiasm. The first image to greet visitors to TraciandTroy.com is a direct representation of that - a classic bride and groom, but caught in the middle of a pose, or possibly a giggle. The site has a vein of understated joy, which makes sense since they used a design by Tonic Site Shop called Lemon Drop, that runs through the font and pops of pale pink. Potential clients will never feel overwhelmed by graphic elements. In fact, the only graphic they will be focused on after scrolling through the site is the "contact us" button.

DESIGNED WITH
LEMON DROP BY TONIC SITE SHOP

COLORS

#404041

#F4E5D9

#E9C2B8

#FFFFFF

#C4C2BF

#DFDEDA

#F7F6F3

TYPEFACES

Raleway Normal

Yellowtail Normal

Oswald

Lato Light

Ubuntu

Libre Baskerville Italic

Montserrat

Playfair Display Italic

Montserrat Bold

Montserrat Normal

Ubuntu Light

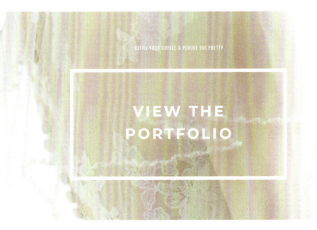

WELCOME, FRIENDS

We're Traci and Troy, a sibling photography team. We strive to create beautiful, timeless imagery that focuses on the wedding story and the people and details that make it so personal to you. We believe your wedding day should be stress free and fun! We seek fun-loving clients who value relationships, and recognize the wedding is only the beginning of a marriage. It is our hope that by the time your wedding day arrives, you see us as new friends and not just hired photographers!

GET TO KNOW US

MEET US — BROWSE OUR WORK

READ THE BLOG — GET IN TOUCH

REFILL YOUR COFFEE & PERUSE THE PRETTY

VIEW THE PORTFOLIO

VIEW THE LATEST ON INSTAGRAM

@TRACIANDTROY

TRACI & TROY

HOME PORTFOLIO
ABOUT EXPERIENCE
BLOG CONTACT

**LOVE IS ALL YOU NEED.
LOVE, AND A PINT OF ICE CREAM.**

We're sibling wedding photographers based in Central Indiana and we love to photograph creative, joyful couples that value meaningful details, natural light, and authentic imagery!

JENNIFER COLE PHOTOGRAPHY

🌐 JENNIFERCOLEPHOTOGRAPHY.COM

First things first, JenniferColePhotography.com is for the easygoing girl ready to show the feminine side of her adventurous soul. This site is a direct reflection of Jennifer's light and ethereal photography, with a keen eye for delicate details. Most importantly, Jennifer wants to convey to her potential clients that her goal is to capture you, and make you comfortable and confident in front of her camera.. "Whatever makes you, you, let's capture that!" Pairing up with Emily Henning, the designer and owner of Seaside Creative, they were able to speak to Jennifer's ideal client through a soft pink palette, clean and beautifully simple navigation, and an attention to type styling. This mirrors the photographer's own thoughtful way that she captures details of her clients, that they will appreciate for decades to come.

DESIGNED BY

EMILY HENNING
SEASIDE CREATIVE

SEASIDECREATIVE.COM

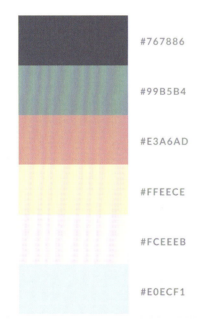

COLORS

- #767886
- #99B5B4
- #E3A6AD
- #FFEECE
- #FCEEEB
- #E0ECF1
- #FFFFFF

TYPEFACES

Playfair Display Italic

Playfair Display

Abel Normal

Karla Normal

JENNIFER COLE
photography

WE LOVE TIMELESS BEAUTY
But live for the authentic everyday moments

WEDDINGS

COUPLES & ENGAGEMENTS

FINE ART PHOTOGRAPHY
SERVING LAS VEGAS, DENVER & BEYOND

THE DETAILS

THE JCOLE EXPERIENCE

WE TREAT OUR CLIENTS LIKE DIAMONDS.

WE ALWAYS HAVE OUR FIRST MEETING WITH OUR CLIENTS IN PERSON.

OVER A DRINK OR A DELICIOUS NUTELLA DESSERT.

I MAY OR MAY NOT SHOW YOU 1,000 PHOTOS OF MY DOG.

I want to get to know you and capture your truth.

There is nothing worse than photographs that you know are staged and don't define you. I want to capture photos that are genuine and authentically you.

Maybe we climb a mountain, go out in a canoe, take a hike, or walk the dogs. Or maybe we dress in Louboutin's and pay Vera

KÉRA PHOTOGRAPHY

🌐 KERAPHOTOGRAPHY.COM

Playful palm fronds are the perfectly cheerful "hello" to any visitor of KeraPhotography.com. These botanical graphics will thus forward serve as ambassadors guiding you through the site, as well as pay homage to Kéra Holzinger's real life home in Florida. With a peppy scripted font of her first name embedded between the fronds, the visitor is greeted in graphic terms that are a direct reflection of Kéra and her craft. Creating visual stories of love for couples who "love uncontrollably and unapologetically," the photographer teamed up with with Ravyn at Three Fifteen Design to collaborate on this visual introduction to Kéra Photography. Adding half frames and shapes with missing pieces, the graphic layout is beautifully different. With sanguine smiles, Kéra and her editorial style will be taking Florida by storm.

DESIGNED BY

RAVYN STADICK
THREE FIFTEEN DESIGN

THREEFIFTEENDESIGN.COM

COLORS

#1B1B1B

#6F6F6F

#FDA099

#FFECEB

#85936E

#DBDBDB

#F1F1F1

#FFFFFF

TYPEFACES

Quicksand Light

Libre Baskerville Italic

Argent Light

Argent Demibold

Visby Light

Visby Bold

Quicksand Normal

Argent Italic

Visby Extra Bold

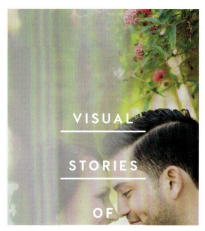

the portfolio

91

CHRONICLES PHOTOGRAPHY

🌐 CHRONICLESPHOTOGRAPHY.COM

Whether it's a classic estate wedding, a ballroom gala, or outdoor celebration, Chronicles Photography has captured them all. So when it came time to choosing what kind of online home to display them in, she chose an elegant design with clean, simple lines and just a touch of color. The emphasis is on the images that would appeal to her ideal bride, a "sentimental romantic who has a classic elegance about her." Dawn Michelle Downey, owner of Chronicles Photography, knows how to bring her brand and her message to her clients so they know exactly what to expect when they hire her. From the initial opening, potential clients are invited to scroll through the luxurious featured weddings, client quotes paired with the reviewer's wedding image, and the most inviting contact page that will have Dawn's inbox constantly full of inquiries.

DESIGNED WITH
GIMLET BY TONIC SITE SHOP

COLORS

#000000

#EE9B86

#FFFFFF

TYPEFACES

Fjalla One

Montserrat

Lato Light

Playfair Display

Quattrocento Sans

Playfair Display Italic

Bodega Script

Live In The Moments
YOU'LL NEVER FORGET...

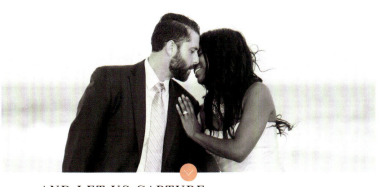

...AND LET US CAPTURE THEM FOR YOU.

Thank you for coming by to learn more about Raleigh Wedding Photographer, Chronicles Photography. Dawn Michelle Downey, owner of Chronicles Photography, is based in Wake Forest, North Carolina. Her photographic specialties are weddings and lifestyle imagery. Though Dawn is based in North Carolina, she is available for continental and international travel. She is now booking weddings and lifestyle sessions for the late 2017 and 2018 season.

Menu: ABOUT   PORTFOLIO   REVIEWS   CONTACT   BLOG

01   *About*

Live In The Moments
YOU'LL NEVER FORGET...

...AND LET US CAPTURE THEM FOR YOU.

Thank you for coming by to learn more about Raleigh Wedding Photographer, Chronicles Photography. Dawn Michelle Downey, owner

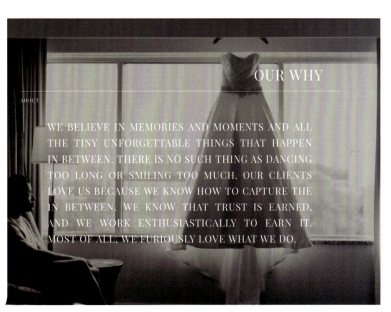

ABOUT

OUR WHY

WE BELIEVE IN MEMORIES AND MOMENTS AND ALL THE TINY UNFORGETTABLE THINGS THAT HAPPEN IN BETWEEN. THERE IS NO SUCH THING AS DANCING TOO LONG OR SMILING TOO MUCH. OUR CLIENTS LOVE US BECAUSE WE KNOW HOW TO CAPTURE THE IN BETWEEN. WE KNOW THAT TRUST IS EARNED, AND WE WORK ENTHUSIASTICALLY TO EARN IT. MOST OF ALL, WE FURIOUSLY LOVE WHAT WE DO.

You and your fiancee are individually unique. A very special thing takes place when two incredibly unique individuals decide to spend eternity together. Recognize that your union is a rare occurrence. Your wedding day will be like no other...

You may have seen our work in:

HUFFINGTON POST   BORROWED & BLUE
MUNALUCHI BRIDAL   BROWN SPARROW WEDDINGS
BLACK BRIDE   WOMAN GETTING MARRIED

I Believe...
...we should work together to create a package that reflects your uniqueness.

Custom collections begin at $1600. Please inquire via the contact link or by clicking HERE.

AURA ELIZABETH PHOTOGRAPHY

🌐 AURAELIZABETH.COM

If you think a classic black and white image would be lost on a site that's been styled with an editorial flair, you would be sadly mistaken. The stark color palette gives the photo a dramatic spotlight. Aura, of Aura Elizabeth Photography, knows how to appeal to her ideal bride. "She appreciates black and white pictures that freeze a moment in time and loves all things classy." When creating her online home, Aura chose to welcome visitors with a whimsical black and white bridal shot to draw her dream client in, however, a quick scroll shows a portfolio packed with color, detail, a behind the scenes video, and an image of Aura dressed in black and white, of course. Her style is a perfect fit for the Tonic Site Shop design that she chose to work with. This site is the perfect blend of classy meets joyful, which is who Aura's ideal bride is.

DESIGNED WITH
JACK ROSE BY TONIC SITE SHOP

COLORS

#000000
#2C3041
#4B5665
#A7A9AB
#0D0D0D
#DFDEDA
#ECEBE8
#FFFFFF

TYPEFACES

Bickham Script
Old Standard TT Italic
England Hand
Libre Baskerville
Sorts Mill Goudy
Libre Baskerville Italic
Old Standard TT
Playfair Display Normal
Ubuntu Medium
Playfair Display Italic
Knockout
Old Standard TT Bold
Ubuntu Bold

AURA ELIZABETH
PHOTOGRAPHY

HOME   MEET AURA   PORTFOLIO   DETAILS   CONTACT   BLOG

For the Undeniably
ROMANTIC AT HEART
THE PORTFOLIO

AURA ELIZABETH
PHOTOGRAPHY

Welcome!
I'm Aura Elizabeth

I'M A LOVER OF ALL THINGS JOYFUL, CLASSY, & LOVELY

Hello there and welcome friend! I'm so glad you're here! I'm Aura Elizabeth and I'm a wedding photographer based in Los Angeles but I love to travel anywhere my business takes me! I'm a small town turned city girl with a love for sweets, sunsets, and classic love stories. I'm passionate about crafting an incredible experience for each of my brides, and I, along with my team, am convinced that we have the sweetest couples EVER. We're for the bride who believes joyful, authentic, & enduring love is worth celebrating. Thank you for stopping by and I hope to have the amazing opportunity to one day hear your love story and share it with the world through the art of photography.

MORE ABOUT AURA

Welcome!

SEE ME IN ACTION

95

CASEY HENDRICKSON PHOTOGRAPHY

CASEYHPHOTOS.COM

Classically elegant, it is easy to be swept away with the unapologetic romance of Casey Hendrickson's online home. Welcomed in with a flourish of fancy font, any potential client will feel embraced by Casey's passion for photographing joyful lovebirds. With sweet couples basking in each other's love, like-minded visitors will get a kick out of finding Harry Potter quotes about love gracefully tucked between photos in a script that has a magic of its own. But Potter isn't the only love Casey managed to work into her brand seamlessly. With help from designer Julie Story, the wedding photographer also found a way to incorporate the true love of her life, her dog Molly. (Complete with her very own precious pooch icons.) WIth all these individual touches, Casey has a uniquely cohesive brand that finally represents herself.

DESIGNED BY

JULIE STORY

JULIE-STORY.COM

COLORS

#EBDDDD

#C5C0BC

#CBBA9E

#000000

#FFFFFF

TYPEFACES

Playfair Display Italic

Miller One

Lato Light

Playfair Display

EB Garamond Normal

WATCH THE
Video

97

MORIAH RIONA

🌐 MORIAHRIONA.COM

What happens when a wedding photographer earns her degree in design? Well, she makes her online home into anything she can dream it to be! And Moriah, of MoriahRiona.com, has done just that. She took her love of classic glamour, paired it with contemporary style, added a pop of sparkle and voilà, c'est chic! Visually, Moriah's site translates to gold trimmings, pink marble accents, and a modern take on leopard spots. But there is so much more. One of the most interesting aspects that Moriah added to her online home is the slow build of design elements. It starts off with just a subtle amount of gold outlines as the visitors watch a black and white film of the photographer at work. Slowly as potential clients are enticed to scroll, Moriah's design elements build and build, leaving visitors wanting more and more Moriah.

DESIGNED FROM SCRATCH
IN SHOWIT

COLORS

#000000
#707070
#BDA474
#F1DAD6
#EBCCC3
#A9A9A9
#ECEBE8
#FFFFFF

TYPEFACES

Raleway Normal

Crimson Text Italic

Crimson Text Semi Bold

Crimson Text Semi Bold Italic

Playfair Display Normal

Raleway Medium

Playfair Display Italic

Crimson Text Bold

Crimson Text Bold Italic

Crimson Text Normal

Raleway Semi Bold

Raleway Bold

MORIAH RIONA

START HERE   FOR BRIDES   FOR PHOTOGRAPHERS   ABOUT   CONTACT   BLOG   SHOP

HELLO GORGEOUS
I'M MORIAH

g photographer and graphic designer who
avel, nerds on art history and drinks way too
uccinos. I'm so glad you're here -- I can't wait
with you.

CHOOSE YOUR EXPERIENCE

MORIAH RIONA
PHOTO | GRAPHIC | DESIGN

HELLO GORGEOUS
I'M MORIAH

A wedding photographer and graphic
designer who loves to travel, nerds on
art history and drinks way too many

for the
BRIDE

PHOTOGRAPHY FOR
the modern romantic with timeless style

For the artist and the fashionista. You are classic glamour meets contemporary. You love deeply and live passionately. You celebrate the big things and cherish the small ones. You are grace, elegance, and sophistication. You are a Moriah Riona Bride.

MORIAH RIONA WEDDINGS >>

WHAT THEY'RE SAYING

"
Moriah captured our wedding
so beautifully...

that my husband and I couldn't even have imagined more perfect photos!!! Her photos were stunning, she was very professional, yet super fun to work with!

CHRISTAN W.
#moriahrionabride

press & features

FOR THE
PHOTOGRAPHER
& creative boss lady

[DREAM BIG]

The Branding Experience by Moriah Riona is not for the hobbyist or the faint of heart. It's for the boss ladies who dream big and have the hustle to back it up.

If you're ready to be brave and invest in your dreams then I'm

99

ZACK DECK MEDIA

 ZACKDECKMEDIA.COM

With an intensity to his work that is one part grit, one part passion, and entirely professional, Zack Deck had a dilemma. Too much design and movement, his images would go unnoticed and it would all be chaos. Too few design elements, the site would just be a picture gallery. The answer was simple, understated black and white to help with a cohesive layout, and blow those images up and let them steal the show. Vertical, a design by Melissa Love at The Design Space, added a straightforward navigation, thin clean framing to draw the eye, and a font that never stands out, but always leads. The visitor, pausing to read a short narrative here and there, will be engrossed in imagining themselves as the subject in every picture. This potential client, "who understands the power of good memories," won't be a "potential" client for much longer.

DESIGNED WITH
VERTICAL BY DESIGN SPACE

COLORS

#000000

#19191A

#4B5665

#70BEBB

#A0D4D2

#DFDEDA

#F9F9F9

#FFFFFF

TYPEFACES

Orbitron Normal

PT Serif

Anton Normal

Righteous Normal

Oxygen Bold

Source Sans Pro

Lato Light

Oxygen Normal

Bentham

PT Serif Italic

Amatic SC Normal

Lato

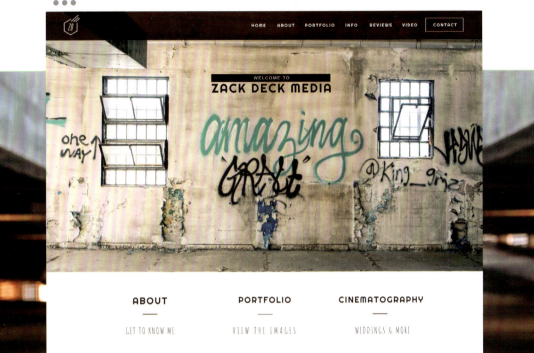

COURTNEY AARON

🌐 COURTNEYAARON.COM

With a thin matte-black frame encapsulating the first full-sized image on CourtneyAaron.com, the whole screen seems to shift focus. The company name and initial information are set in a classic font, which further exaggerates the unexpected intensity of Courtney's site, a design from Tonic Site Shop called Amaretto Sour. It's the cheerfully scripted "welcome to" that lets potential clients know they are in for a real treat as they keep scrolling. As a "fellow camera dodger," potential clients will warm up to Courtney immediately. Whether they choose to learn more about their future photographer, take a dreamy trip through her portfolio, or get completely lost in the fully-engaging site, each visitor must not miss the finale of film hidden at the end where the full picture of the Courtney Aaron Photography experience lays.

DESIGNED WITH
AMARETTO SOUR BY TONIC SITE SHOP

COLORS

#000000

#F7F7F7

#FDFDFD

#FFFFFF

TYPEFACES

Didot Regular

Oswald Normal

Libre Baskerville

Lato Light

Lato Bold

Playfair Display Italic

Lato Normal

Manus

Crimson Text Normal

Playfair Display

HOME   PORTFOLIO   ABOUT ME   COURTNEY AARON   EXPERIENCE   CONTACT   BLOG

welcome to
COURTNEY AARON
Where old souls with big hearts can be at ease having their most meaningful moments captured naturally.

PHOTOGRAPHY BASED IN LAKE TAHOE & PHILADELPHIA

SCROLL TO EXPLORE

well, hello. i'm
COURTNEY
PHOTOGRAPHER. MOM. FELLOW CAMERA-DODGER.

Eleven years ago I slung a camera strap around my neck, and I've been capturing moments and memories that will be cherished for generations to come ever since. My goal? Put you at ease in front of the camera and document what matters and giving you something timeless in a fleeting world.

READ MORE ▸

the portfolio
FEATURED WORK

CHIC HOBOKEN ENGAGEMENT
JILL + BRANDON

VALHALLA AT LAKE TAHOE
TARA + CHANCE

ROMANTIC MOUNTAIN SESSION
BRITTANY + DANIEL

I.
RECENTLY ON THE BLOG

MOUNTAIN MEADOW FAMILY SESSION

The Burton Family came to Tahoe for one last family session in the Sierras before they made their big move north to Oregon. A pretty enchanting evening to

CASEY CHIBIRKA PHOTOGRAPHY

🌐 CASEYCHIBIRKA.COM

Having discovered her passion for photography in junior high, Casey Chibirka has spent her life devoted to the fine art. While the subject of her photography switched throughout her education, she has now found a place and people that inspire her like no other. "My inspiration comes from the land, or *aina* in Hawaiian." As an island dweller, Hawaii bleeds into every aspect of her business, and therefore needed to play a key role in her online home as well. From her sweet botanical hand-drawn logo, to every one of her images, Casey targets her ideal client, "anyone who isn't afraid to get sandy, wet, and possibly muddy…who understands the process it takes to truly capture a moment in time." After reading more about Casey and her philosophies, that free-spirit bride will be sending an "aloha" in hopes of a booking!

DESIGNED WITH
CARSON BY NORTHFOLK & CO.

COLORS

#4F5258
#A9A198
#FBF5F3
#D3CBC6
#FFFFFF

TYPEFACES

Cormorant Italic

Cormorant Normal

Bodoni FLF

Melike Letter

Cormorant Semi Bold

I	II	III	IV	V	VI
HOME	BIO	DETAILS	WORK	BLOG	INQUIRE

Meet the Artist

Aloha, I am Casey Chibirka, the photographer behind the lens. I am a Wedding and Fine Art Portrait Photographer. Specializing in capturing love and family.

My love for photography began the traditional way. I purchased my first film camera in middle school and signed myself up for darkroom photography classes. Being in the darkroom and creating art through my lens gave me a sense of self. I knew that photography was what I wanted to do for the rest of my life. I later studied Photography in Philadelphia at *Antonelli Institute of Art & Photography* and fell even more in love with the art.

After finishing my studies, I established roots on Kauai. It was here on the island I learned about the Hawaiian principles of life, *mana*, being a principle that really stuck out to me. And is now a quality I live by.

About Mana

Meet the Artist

Browse Our Galleries

01 PORTRAIT
02 ELOPEMENT
03 WEDDINGS

testimonial

"AN EXCELLENT PHOTOGRAPHER & TRULY

United

TRANSFORM YOUR PHOTOGRAPHY BUSINESS
IN 4 DAYS

 CONNECT   **GROW**   **STRENGTHEN**

Connect with industry leaders and like-minded creatives in an encouraging and intimate environment.

Gain new perspective and clarity to fall in love with your business all over again.

Strengthen your business and hone your craft through breakout sessions and educational photo shoots.

LEARN MORE
REGISTER → **SHOWIT.CO/UNITED**

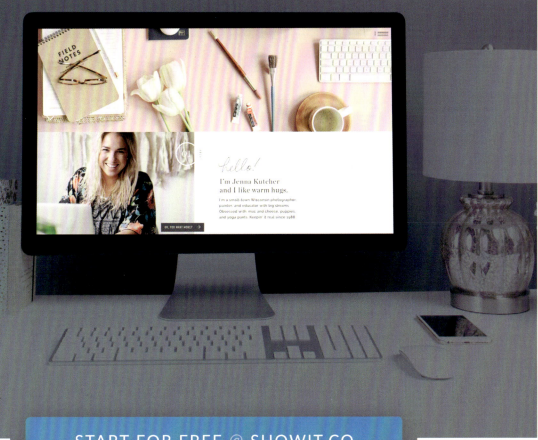

BE THE SOURCE OF INSPIRATION

Get featured in the next issue

APPLY @ SHOWIT.CO/SPARK